Robot
COMPETITIONS

BY CHRISTOPHER FOREST

CAPSTONE PRESS
a capstone imprint

Edge Books are published by Capstone Press,
1710 Roe Crest Drive, North Mankato, Minnesota 56003
www.capstonepub.com

Library of Congress Cataloging-in-Publication Data
Forest, Christopher.
  Robot competitions / by Christopher Forest.
     pages cm.—(Edge books. Robots)
  Includes bibliographical references and index.
  ISBN 978-1-4296-9920-4 (library binding)
  ISBN 978-1-62065-782-9 (paperback)
  ISBN 978-1-4765-1559-5 (ebook PDF)
1. Robotics—Competitions—Juvenile literature. 2. Robots—Juvenile literature. I.
Title.
  TJ211.2.F66 2013
  629.8'92079—dc23   2012026442

Summary: Describes a variety of robot competitions held in the United States and
around the world.

Editorial Credits
Christopher L. Harbo, editor; Ted Williams, designer; Eric Gohl, media researcher;
Laura Manthe, production specialist

Photo Credits
Alamy: Jeff Greenberg, 10–11; AP Images: Jeff Klein, 9, Koji Sasahara, 21, University
of Florida/Joe Richard, 16–17; NASA: JPL-Caltech, 13; Newscom: EPA/Ingo Wagner,
23, Feature Photo Service, 11, picture-alliance/dpa/Jens Wolf, cover, 22, Unimedia
Images, Inc./DreamWorks Pictures, 7, ZUMA Press, 14, ZUMA Press/Bruce Bisping,
29; RoboGames: Dave Schumaker, 5, Sam Coniglio, 19; Stefan Hrabar: CSIRO, 24, 27

Design Elements
Shutterstock

Capstone Press thanks professor Nicola J. Ferrier from the Department of Mechanical
Engineering at the University of Wisconsin-Madison for her help with this book.

Printed in the United States of America in Stevens Point, Wisconsin.
092012   006937WZS13

Table of
CONTENTS

Let the Games Begin!

Imagine a future in which humans aren't needed for the jobs we do today. Passenger planes flying without pilots. Cars driving themselves. Robots cleaning your room. Does this sound like a science fiction movie? Maybe, but some of these things are a lot closer than you think.

Robots already help people in many ways. They build cars in factories. They help astronauts working in space. They even do small tasks in people's homes. But robots aren't just all work and no play.

Each year robots from around the world show their fun side in robot competitions. Some competitions pit robot against robot in fierce battles. Others challenge robots to race through mazes or complete rescue missions. Robots even compete in sporting events such as soccer, boxing, and kung fu. No matter how robots compete, these events test the limits of robotics.

Sparks fly as two combat robots smash together at RoboGames in San Mateo, California.

Competitions Past and Present

Robot competitions date back to 1989 at MileHiCon in Denver, Colorado. During this science fiction convention, several hand-built robots clashed in the Critter Crunch. This event was a winner-take-all battle. Robot battled robot until the last one standing won. The Critter Crunch launched an international sensation. Soon, robots were racing, flying, and playing sports in competitions around the world.

Today robot competitions are common. Many colleges, high schools, and middle schools have robotics clubs and teams that compete. Companies and organizations also host contests. These companies view competitions as a way to inspire future scientists and **engineers**.

 engineer—someone trained to design, modify, or build machines, vehicles, devices, materials, and structures

ROBOT FACT

The winner of the Critter Crunch was a 19-pound (8.6-kilogram) robot called Thing One. It beat other robots in the competition while shooting a can of Silly String.

Lights, Camera, Robot Action!

Robot contests have been a hit in both TV shows and movies. TV shows like *BattleBots* and *Robot Wars* have shown the thrill of battling robots. *BattleBots* aired from 2000 to 2002 with footage from several U.S. BattleBot competitions. *Robot Wars* was a British robot-fighting game show that aired from 1998 to 2003. The 2011 movie *Real Steel* featured robots battling in the boxing ring.

In the 2011 movie *Real Steel*, a robot named Atom is trained to box.

U.S. Competitions

Robot competitions have come a long way since MileHiCon in 1989. Since then, the number of contests in the United States has skyrocketed. These competitions include all-out battles, underwater exploration, and a variety of sporting events.

BattleBots

Imagine two robots locked in battle. Sparks fly as they crash. They cling together and slam each other against the wall until one robot can no longer move. Welcome to BattleBots, a competition that has pitted robot against robot since 1999.

ROBOT FACT

The 2011 BattleBots National Championship was held in Miami, Florida. During the competition, a high school team's robot named Fluffy De Large fought and beat a professional team's robot named Witch Doctor.

A robot with comedian Jay Leno's face named Chin-Killa flips a robot named Ginsu during a BattleBots competition.

BattleBots has three divisions. The first division includes professional robot designers. College students compete in the second division. The third division allows high school and middle school students to battle their robots. All three divisions can compete in either 15-pound (6.8-kg) or 120-pound (54-kg) weight classes.

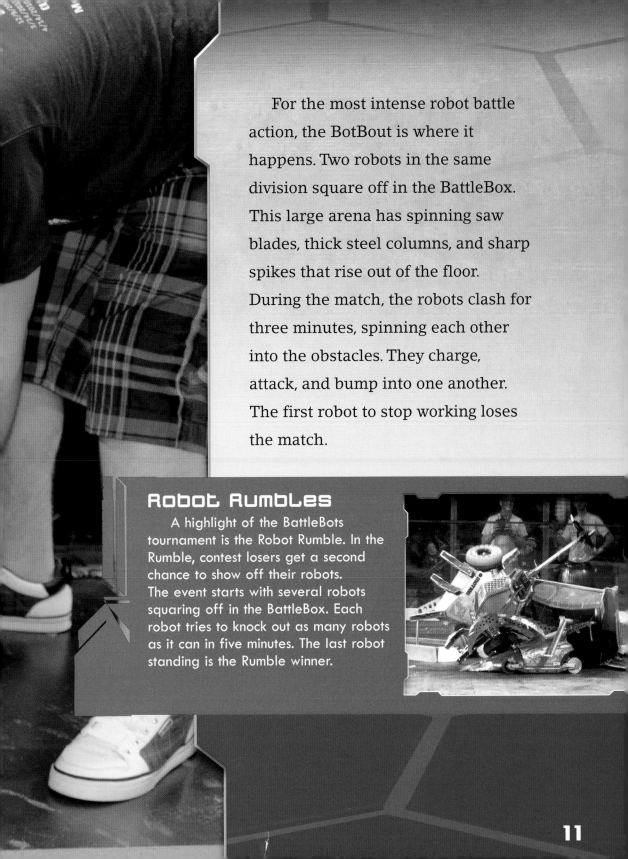

For the most intense robot battle action, the BotBout is where it happens. Two robots in the same division square off in the BattleBox. This large arena has spinning saw blades, thick steel columns, and sharp spikes that rise out of the floor. During the match, the robots clash for three minutes, spinning each other into the obstacles. They charge, attack, and bump into one another. The first robot to stop working loses the match.

Robot Rumbles

A highlight of the BattleBots tournament is the Robot Rumble. In the Rumble, contest losers get a second chance to show off their robots. The event starts with several robots squaring off in the BattleBox. Each robot tries to knock out as many robots as it can in five minutes. The last robot standing is the Rumble winner.

FIRST Robotics Competition

The For Inspiration and Recognition of Science and Technology (FIRST) Robotics Competition focuses on student robot designers. Started in 1992, FIRST competition organizers hope to get students interested in science, engineering, and technology. Today more than 50 regional competitions and one championship event are held each year. Teams are made up of students ages 6 to 9, 9 to 14, and 14 to 18. These teams design robots that solve problems or complete tasks. Most robots must be **autonomous**.

 autonomous—able to control oneself; autonomous robots are not operated remotely by a person

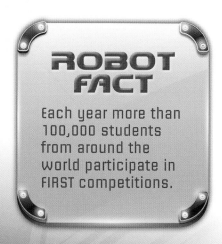

ROBOT FACT

Each year more than 100,000 students from around the world participate in FIRST competitions.

During past competitions, robots have collected tennis balls, stacked storage bins, and gathered soccer balls. Robots sometimes work together as teams to test their abilities against other teams. Individual robots earn points based on tasks they finish. In 2012 the theme of the FIRST competition was Rebound Rumble. Teams scored points with robots that could shoot basketballs into hoops.

A Navy diver helps lift a robot named Stingray from the practice pool during a 2009 RoboSub competition.

RoboSub

Not all robot competitions take place on land. RoboSub in San Diego, California, takes robots underwater. This yearly competition is held by the U.S. Office of Naval Research and the Association of Unmanned Vehicle Systems International. Competitors develop robot submarines for underwater exploration and national defense.

ROBOT FACT

The U.S. Office of Naval Research also holds competitions for elementary and middle school students. These students can design robots called SeaPerches that explore underwater.

For RoboSub, high school and college teams build unmanned underwater robot vehicles. Team members **tele-operate** these subs on missions in a large pool. The missions are designed to challenge the robot submarines and their teams with a variety of tasks. These tasks include striking underwater buoys, passing through an obstacle course, and firing torpedoes. The subs must also drop **markers** and capture a plastic hoop called a laurel wreath.

 tele-operate—to control a machine from a distance
marker—an object used to show a position

A robot from the University of Florida makes a practice run before a RoboSub competition.

Each RoboSub competition has a semifinal and final round. For both rounds, teams have 20 minutes of competition time. Five minutes are used to prepare the sub for its mission. Then the sub has 15 minutes to complete its tasks. Teams earn points for how well their subs complete each task. Points are also awarded for how fast the subs complete their missions. Teams with the highest points in the semifinals advance to the finals. The team that earns the most points in the finals wins the competition.

RoboGames

Soccer. Boxing. Weight lifting. No, this isn't the Olympics. It's RoboGames. Held in San Mateo, California, RoboGames is open to any robot builder. It gives builders more than 50 different events to choose from.

RoboGames has two robot categories, autonomous and tele-operated. During competitions, robots may shoot flames, do backflips, or perform tasks such as pushing tubes or climbing stairs. Competitions include **humanoid** robots competing in soccer matches. The Art Bot–Musical competition has robots playing instruments. Robot hockey pits two robot teams against each other in a street hockey game.

 humanoid—having human form or characteristics; a humanoid robot is shaped somewhat like a human but is clearly a robot

ROBOT FACT

According to the *Guinness Book of World Records*, RoboGames is the largest robot-based event in the world.

Mech Wars

Mech Warfare is a popular RoboGames event. This contest features robots that attack each other like monsters in a movie. The robots must walk on two to six legs while moving through a miniature city. Weapons may include mini flamethrowers and mini rockets. The last robot standing wins.

International Competitions

The popularity of robot competitions has spread around the world. In Japan, sumo wrestling robots push each other out of wrestling rings. In Europe and Asia, robot soccer matches test the athletic limits of robotics. Australia hosts a competition with flying robots.

Robot Sumo Wrestling

Each year FujiSoft, Inc. (FSI) hosts the FSI-All Japan Robot-Sumo Tournament. It challenges robot builders to design robots to take part in a **simulated** sumo match. Sumo robots must fit into a box 7.8 inches (20 centimeters) wide and deep. They can weigh no more than 6.6 pounds (3 kg). In some divisions, people tele-operate the robots from a distance. In others, the robots control themselves.

 simulate—to mimic or act like something else

Sumo robots Brutal Tank (left) and Satoru (right) use raw power to try to push each other out of the ring.

The contest looks like a real sumo match. Two robots face off in a ring. Each robot tries to score a point by pushing the other robot out of the ring. Robots may tip during a match, but are allowed to right themselves if they're inside the ring. The first robot to win two out of three matches wins the game.

RoboCup

Each year robots and soccer come together in the RoboCup tournament. This international competition is held in a different country each year. It brings together more than 100 teams that design autonomous robots. Two teams of robots play soccer against each other with the winner moving to another round.

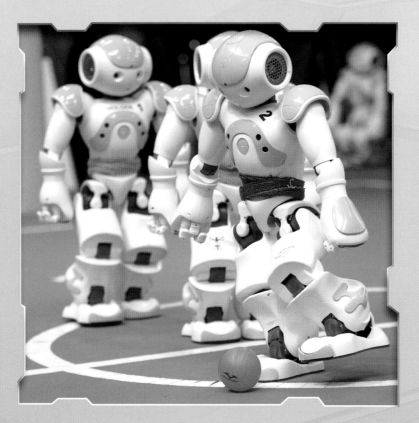

A humanoid robot in the standard platform league balances on one foot as it prepares to kick the ball.

Robots in the small size league charge the net as they try to score a goal.

RoboCup teams fall into one of five major categories. In the small size and the middle size leagues, teams of rolling robots play soccer with an orange golf ball. The humanoid league uses robots that walk, run, kick, and see a ball with humanlike bodies and senses. The standard platform league also uses humanoid robots. But these robots have the same design to allow teams to focus on developing software. The simulation league uses computer programs instead of mechanical robots. It features teams that program players to simulate a soccer game on a computer. The ultimate goal of all of these leagues is to develop robots that act like humans. By 2050, RoboCup hopes to have robots that can compete against human World Cup soccer champions.

In the Airborne Delivery Challenge, teams try to drop an emergency rescue package to Outback Joe.

UAV Challenge

Where can you see the Australian **outback** and robot airplanes at the same time? At the yearly UAV Challenge–Outback Rescue held in Queensland, Australia. This robot competition encourages interest in unmanned airborne vehicles (UAVs).

The UAV Challenge is split into two competitions. The Airborne Delivery Challenge is open to Australian high school students. The Search and Rescue Challenge is open to university students and professionals from Australia and around the world. Both challenges use a 110-pound (50-kg) **mannequin** named Outback Joe.

outback—the flat desert areas of Australia; few people live in the outback

mannequin—a life-sized dummy of a human

For the Airborne Delivery Challenge, Outback Joe sits between two tall hurdles. Teams fly their robotic airplanes over the hurdles to drop an emergency package to Outback Joe. Each team gets 20 minutes to make up to three drop attempts. Points are awarded for how close to Outback Joe the rescue package lands. The team with the highest point total wins $8,000 (AU).

The Search and Rescue Challenge, held every two years, is even more difficult. In this challenge, Outback Joe is "lost" in a rural area. To "save" him, teams must use their planes to search for him from the air. Once they find Outback Joe, their planes must drop a rescue package of water as close to him as possible. During the competition, teams can fly no higher than 1,500 feet (460 meters) before getting to Joe. Teams earn points on a flight demonstration video, a presentation about their flight plan, and their flight performance. The grand prize of the competition is $50,000 (AU).

A UAV prepares for takeoff at the Airborne Delivery Challenge.

ROBOT FACT

The Search and Rescue Challenge is considered one of the most difficult robot competitions in the world. Between 2007 and 2011, no team had completed the challenge to claim the grand prize.

Competing for the Future

Robot competitions are not only fun, but also important to the future of robotics. Competitions show that robots are more than just machines that perform work. They allow robot builders to expand their ideas for robots and work together on new designs. Competitions also inspire young robot builders. They encourage many students to go into robotics education and careers.

Robot competitions often lead to improvements in technology. Robots that fight fires, explore oceans, and fly through the air have all been developed from contests. Contests have also helped military and public safety workers design lifesaving robots.

The robots of tomorrow depend on the competitions held today. Because these competitions are very common, you can probably find one in your area to enter. Grab some tools, get some metal and plastic, and put together some gears, wires, and wheels. The next groundbreaking robot might just be the one you invent.

A high school robotics team from Chaska, Minnesota, operates its robot at a FIRST Robotics Competition.

Glossary

autonomous (aw-TAH-nuh-muhss)—able to control oneself; autonomous robots are not operated remotely by a person

engineer (en-juh-NEER)—someone trained to design, modify, or build machines, vehicles, devices, materials, and structures

humanoid (HYOO-muh-noid)—having human form or characteristics; a humanoid robot is shaped somewhat like a human but is clearly a robot

mannequin (MAN-i-kin)—a life-sized dummy of a human

marker (MAR-kur)—an object used to show a position

outback (OUT-bak)—the flat desert areas of Australia; few people live in the outback

simulate (SIM-yoo-layt)—to mimic or act like something else

tele-operate (TEL-uh-OP-uh-rate)—to control a machine from a distance

Read More

Brasch, Nicolas. *Robots of the Future*. Discovery Education: Technology. New York: PowerKids Press, 2013.

Hyland, Tony. *How Robots Work*. Robots and Robotics. North Mankato, Minn.: Smart Apple Media, 2008.

Rau, Dana Meachen. *Robots*. Surprising Science. New York: Marshall Cavendish Benchmark, 2011.

Internet Sites

FactHound offers a safe, fun way to find Internet sites related to this book. All of the sites on FactHound have been researched by our staff.

Here's all you do:

Visit *www.facthound.com*

Type in this code: 9781429699204

Check out projects, games and lots more at
www.capstonekids.com

Index